I WAIT FOR YOU

Jesus' Lament Over Man's Indifference

I WAIT FOR YOU

Jesus' Lament Over
Man's Indifference

Selected and arranged from
The Way of Divine Love
of Sr. Josefa Menéndez

*"You will never regret any
sacrifice you have made for
Me during your life"*

—Words of Jesus, p. 35

TAN Books
Charlotte, North Carolina

Nihil Obstat: Patrieius Morris, S.T.D., L.S.S.
Censor Deputatus

Imprimatur: E. Morrogh Bernard, Vic. Gen.
Westmonasterii, die 5a Maii, 1953

The material in this book was originally published in 1949 by Sands & Co. (Publishers), Ltd., 79 Larmans Road, Enfield, Middlesex, England under the title of *The Way of Divine Love*.

Copyright © 1985 by TAN Books.

ISBN: 978-0-89555-285-3

Printed and bound in the United States of America.

TAN Books
Charlotte, North Carolina
www.TANBooks.com
2011

INTRODUCTION

The purpose of this pamphlet is to rekindle devotion to the Blessed Sacrament, and to do so by adducing the testimony of Jesus Himself, gathered from His revelations to Sister Josefa Menéndez in the early part of the twentieth century—practically in our own times.

All the pages of this pamphlet have been excerpted from *The Way of Divine Love*, that classic account of Jesus' numerous appearances and revelations to Sister Josefa, Though they may seem to be randomly chosen, they have one thing in common. In them all there is a reference to Mass, Holy Communion or the Blessed Sacrament. In most, Jesus Himself speaks, instructing Josefa, and through her, the whole world.

No effort has been made to edit them in any way or to point out the relevant passages. It is hoped that the cumulative effect of Our Lord's words on the subject of the Eucharist will convince the reader that Jesus very much wants the faithful to keep Him company in the tabernacle and that something must be done to revive devotion to the Blessed Sacrament. If He complained bitterly in the first quarter of this century of being neglected and ignored, who can gauge the depth of the hurt He must feel today, in the last several decades when the routine closing of churches during the day is simply accepted as a sign of the times. The message of this pamphlet, then, is that Jesus Himself wants to rekindle devotion to the Blessed Sacrament.

If the reader who is unacquainted with *The Way of Divine Love* will find his appetite whetted by these few sample pages, he will find it a tremendous added spiritual bonus to go to their source for the full story of Jesus' incredible number of appearances and conversations with this humble Spanish Lay Sister who lived her short Religious life in France and died in 1923 at the age of 33. For no other Catholic book we know of carries the impact of The Way of Divine Love!

The Publishers

A BRIEF BIOGRAPHICAL SKETCH OF SISTER JOSEFA MENÉNDEZ

Josefa Menéndez was born in Madrid, Spain on February 4, 1890. On her thirtieth birthday, February 4, 1920, she entered the Society of the Sacred Heart as a lay or coadjutrix sister in its convent in Poitiers, France, known as Les Feuillants.

In the spring of 1920, while still a postulant, she was not only strongly tempted to leave the convent and return home but actually was visibly tormented by evil spirits. At this time also, Jesus began to draw her into an intimate union with Him, including visions of His Sacred Heart and speaking to her words that, under the guidance of her superiors, she wrote down and which have been preserved in the form of a book called *The Way of Divine Love.*

Her clothing day was July 16, 1920, when she received the habit of the Society of the Sacred Heart. On July 16, 1922, she made her First Vows, and she died on December 29, 1923, after less than four years of religious life.

When, in 1938, the story of her life was published in *An Appeal for Love*, the shorter version that preceded *The Way of Divine Love*, then Cardinal Pacelli, later to become Pope Pius XII, who was Protector of the Society of the Sacred Heart in Rome, gave his blessing to it in a short letter in which he wrote as follows:

Very Reverend Mother,

I have no doubt whatever that the publication of these pages, filled as they are with the great love which His grace inspired in His very humble servant, Maria Josefa Menéndez, will be agreeable to His Sacred Heart.

May they efficaciously contribute to develop in many souls a confidence ever more complete and loving in the infinite mercy of this Divine Heart towards poor sinners, such as we all are.

These are the good wishes which with my blessing, I send you and all the Society of the Sacred Heart.

E. Card. Pacelli

DECLARATION

In obedience to the decrees of Pope Urban VIII and other sovereign Pontiffs, the writer declares that the graces and other supernatural facts related in this volume as witnessing to the sanctity of Servants of God, other than those canonized or beatified by the Church, rest on human authority alone; and in regard thereto, as in all things else, the writer submits herself without reserve to the infallible judgment of the Apostolic See which alone has power and authority to pronounce as to whom rightly belong the character and title of Saint or Blessed.

I WAIT FOR YOU

In the afternoon on Holy Thursday, April 13th, 1922, she wrote:

"I was in the chapel at about half-past three when I saw before me a personage clothed like Our Lord, rather taller, very beautiful and with a wonderful expression of peace on his face which was most attractive. His vesture was of a dark reddish purple. He held in his hand the Crown of Thorns, just like the one Our Lord used to bring me long ago.

"'I am the Disciple of the Lord,' he said, 'John the Evangelist, and I bring you one of the Master's most precious jewels.'

"He gave me the Crown and himself placed it on my head."

Josefa was at first rather startled at this unexpected apparition, but she gained assurance through the feeling of intense peace which took possession of her. She ventured to confide in the saintly visitor, telling him of the anguish the ill-treatment of the devil caused her.

"'Have no fear,' was the reply. 'Your soul is a lily which is kept by Jesus in His Heart—I am sent to make you acquainted with some of the feelings that overwhelmed His Heart on this great day:

"'Love was about to part Him from His disciples, after it had baptized Him in a baptism of blood. But love urged Him to remain with them, and it was love that made Him conceive the idea of the Blessed Sacrament.

"'What a struggle then arose in His Heart. He thought of how He would rest in pure souls, but also how His Passion would be carried on in hearts sullied by sin.

"'How His Heart thrilled at the thought of the moment, then approaching, when He would go to the Father, but It was crushed with sorrow at the sight of one of the Twelve, one specially chosen, who was to deliver Him up to death, and at the knowledge that for the first time His Blood was to prove useless to save a soul.

"'How His Heart wore itself out in love! But the want of correspondence to grace of those so beloved plunged It into dire distress . . . and what of the indifference and coldness of so many chosen souls?'

"With these words he was gone."

This heavenly visitation upheld her courage for a time, as it brought so forcibly before her mind the call to reparation by which the Holy Eucharist appeals to consecrated souls.

On Sunday, February 25th, Jesus visited her in her cell very early in the morning.

"Why do you fear?" He said gently to her. "Perhaps, because you have still many imperfections, but there is no question of the sins the devil accuses you of . . . Yes, renew your vows strengthening the bonds that unite us . . . And now, Josefa, do not forget that you are but a tool, and a very useless and wretched one.

"Kiss the ground and write . . . for we are going on with Love's secrets.

"I will tell you My reasons for washing the feet of My apostles before the Last Supper.

"In the first place I would teach souls how pure they must be to receive Me in Holy Communion.

"I also wished to remind those who would have the misfortune to sin that they can always recover their innocence through the Sacrament of Penance.

"And I washed the feet of My apostles with My own hands, so that those who have consecrated themselves to apostolic work may follow My example, and treat sinners with humility and gentleness, as also all others that are entrusted to their care.

"I girded Myself with a white linen cloth to remind them that apostles need to be girded with abnegation and mortification, if they hope to exert any real influence on souls . . .

"I wished also to teach them that mutual charity which is ever ready to excuse the faults of others, to conceal them and extenuate them, and never to reveal them.

"Lastly, the water poured on the feet of My apostles denotes the zeal which burned in My Heart for the salvation of the world.

"The hour of Redemption was at hand. My Heart could no longer restrain its love for mankind nor bear the thought of leaving them orphans.

"So, to prove My tender love for them and in order to remain always with them till time has ceased to be, I resolved to become their food, their support, their life, their all. Could I but make known to all souls the loving sentiments with which My Heart overflowed at My Last Supper, when I instituted the Sacrament of the Holy Eucharist . . . !

"My glance ranged across the ages, and I saw the multitudes who would receive My Body and Blood, and all the good It would effect . . . how many hearts I saw that from Its contact would bud forth virginity! . . . and how many others that It would awaken to deeds of charity and zeal! . . . How many martyrs of love did I see . . . How many souls who had been enfeebled by sin and the violence of passion would come back to their allegiance and recover their spiritual energy by partaking of this Bread of the strong! . . .

"Who can describe the overwhelming emotions that filled My Soul? Joy, love, tenderness . . . but, alas, bitter sorrow also . . .

"Later I shall continue, Josefa. Go now in My peace; console Me, and do not be afraid; the wellspring of My Blood is not exhausted, and It will cleanse your soul."

Here Jesus Stopped.

"Adieu, kiss the ground. I shall return."

"The Holy Eucharist is the invention of Love, but how few souls correspond to that love which spends and consumes itself for them!"—Our Lord to Josefa, March 2nd, 1923

On the First Friday, March 2nd, at about nine o'clock, Josefa, active and alert, hurried to her workroom. She had waited long for the coming of Our Lord in her cell, but once again He had not come. She wrote in all sincerity: "I was rather glad to have the time, for I had a lot of sewing to do . . . At times I am haunted by the idea that I do no work at all, and that I am of no use, what with all those things . . ."

This was a return of the old temptation which the devil never failed to suggest to her eager and devoted nature.

"On reaching the foot of the 'Saint Michael' staircase, I came face to face with Jesus. He stopped me and said: 'Josefa, where are you going?'

"'I am on my way to iron the uniforms in the linen-room, Lord.'

"'Go to your cell,' He said, 'for I want you to write.'"

She smothered the secret wish she had to get on with her work, and went upstairs and found that Jesus had already preceded her.

"Who made you, Josefa?" was His first question after she had renewed her vows.

"Thou, Lord."

"Has anyone shown you more love than I? . . . Who has forgiven you so often as I, and who will do so again? . . ."

Full of shame, she was at His feet in an instant.

"Yes, humble yourself, Josefa; kiss the ground, and never resist My will. Now write for My souls:

"I want to tell them of the poignant sorrows which filled My Heart at the Last Supper. If it was bliss for Me to think of all those to whom I should be both Companion and Heavenly Food, of all who would surround Me to the End of

Time with adoration, reparation, and love . . . this in no wise diminished My grief at the many who would leave Me deserted in My tabernacle and who would not even believe in My Real Presence.

"Into how many hearts defiled by sin would I not have to enter . . . and how often this profanation of My Body and Blood would serve for their ultimate condemnation . . .

"Sacrileges and outrages, and all the nameless abominations to be committed against Me, passed before My eyes . . . the long, lonely hours of the day and of the night in which I would remain alone on the altars . . . and the multitudes who would not heed the appeals of My Heart . . .

"Ah! Josefa, let the thoughts of My Heart sink deep into yours.

"It is love for souls that keeps Me a Prisoner in the Blessed Sacrament. I stay there that all may come and find the comfort they need in the tenderest of Hearts, the best of Fathers, the most faithful of Friends, who will never abandon them.

"The Holy Eucharist is the invention of Love . . . Yet how few souls correspond to that love which spends and consumes itself for them!

"I live in the midst of sinners that I may be their life, their physician, and the remedy of the diseases bred by corrupt nature. And in return they forsake, insult and despise Me! . . .

"Poor pitiable sinners, do not turn away from Me . . . Day and night I am on the watch for you in the tabernacle. I will not reproach you . . . I will not cast your sins in your face . . . But I will wash them in My Blood and in My Wounds. No need to be afraid . . . come to Me . . . If you but knew how dearly I love you.

"And you, dear souls, why this coldness and indifference on your part? . . . Do I not know that family cares . . . household concerns . . . and the requirements of your position in life . . . make continual calls upon you? . . . But cannot you spare a few minutes in which to come and prove your affection and your gratitude? Do not allow yourselves to be involved in useless and incessant cares, but spare a few moments to visit and receive this Prisoner of Love! . . .

"Were you weak or ill in body surely you would find time to see a doctor who would cure you? . . . Come, then, to One who is able to give both strength and health to your soul, and bestow the alms of love on this Divine Prisoner who watches for you, calls for you and longs to see you at His side.

"When about to institute the Blessed Sacrament, Josefa, these were My feelings, but I have not yet told you what My Heart felt at the thought of My chosen souls; My religious, My priests . . . but I will tell you all this later on. Go, now, and do not forget that My Heart loves you . . . and, Josefa, do you love Me? . . ."

It was by her courageous fidelity, more than by her words of love, that Josefa replied to this question of her Master. During the following night, which was more full of pain than ever, she gathered from the blasphemies of the devil that the three souls so specially dear to the Heart of Jesus and for which she had suffered so much during the past fortnight were about to return to Him. This encouraged her.

On the evening of the First Saturday, March 3rd, she was in adoration before the Blessed Sacrament, when Our Lord appeared to her with His Heart all gloriously aflame.

"Josefa," He said with eager voice, "let Me rest a while in you, let Me tell you of My joy: those three souls that I had entrusted to you have come back to Me. . . .

And He continued: "My Cross is heavy. . . . That is why I come here to rest and to give a share of it to each of My well-beloved souls. . . . My Heart is in search of victims to lead the world to love, and I find them here."

With what joy Josefa joined in her Master's exultation. She offered Him all the desires of the house, which she knew were sincere and ardent, that His Heart might find comfort and that many erring souls might return to Him. Then, as she could not forget what Our Lord dictated to her yesterday, she asked Him if He would not tell her for His chosen souls what He expected of them in the Holy Eucharist.

"Yes," He answered, "I want to tell you this, that My best-loved and specially favored souls, My priests and My consecrated nuns, may learn it through you. If their infidelities wound Me deeply, their love consoles and delights My Heart to such a degree that I, so to speak, forget the sins of many others on their account."

There followed a few days of interruption; then once more on Tuesday, March 6th, Jesus came at eight o'clock in the morning.

"'Josefa, are you expecting Me?' He asked. 'I am going to reveal to you the greatest mystery of My love . . . of love for My chosen consecrated souls. Begin by kissing the ground. . . . When about to institute the Holy Eucharist, I saw the privileged throng who would be nourished by My Body and Blood; some would find there the remedy for their short-comings, others consuming fire for their imperfections. . . . I likewise saw them gathered round Me as in a garden, each separately rejoicing Me with her flowers and their scent. . . . As a vivifying sun, My sacred Body gave them life, and warmed their cold hearts. . . . To some I went for comfort, to others for refuge, to others again for rest. . . . Would that all these cherished souls knew how easily they can console Me, harbor Me, or give rest to Me their God.

"'It is this infinitely loving God who after freeing you from the slavery of sin has given you the incomparable grace of your vocation and has mysteriously attracted you into the enclosed garden of His delights. This God who is your Savior has made Himself your Bridegroom.

"'And He Himself feeds you with His immaculate Flesh and slakes your thirst with His Blood. If you are sick, He will be your physician; come to Him, He will cure you. If you are cold, come to Him; He will warm you. In Him you will find rest and happiness, so do not wander away from Him, for He is life, and when He asks you to comfort Him, do not sadden Him by a refusal. . . .

"'Alas, what sorrow it is to see so many who have been endowed with My choicest graces become a cause of pain to My Sacred Heart! Am I not always the same? . . . Have I changed? . . . No, My love is unalterable and will endure to the End of Time with the same tenderness and predilection.

"'That you are unworthy I well know; but not for that do I turn away from you. On the contrary, with anxious solicitude I look for your coming, that I may not only ease your troubles, but also grant you many favors.

"If I ask your love, do not refuse it. It is so easy to love Love itself.

"'If I should ask you for things that cost, know that at the same time I will give you all the grace and strength you need to conquer yourself.

"I hope to find in you My comfort, therefore have I chosen you. Open your whole soul to Me, and if you are conscious of having nothing worthy of Me, say with humility and trust: Lord, Thou knowest both the flowers and fruits of my garden . . . come and teach me how I may grow, what will please Thee most. To one who speaks in this way and has a genuine desire of showing love, I answer: Beloved, if such is your desire, suffer *Me* to grow them for you . . . let Me delve and dig in your garden . . . let Me clear the ground of those sinewy roots that obstruct it and which you have not the strength to pull up. . . . Maybe I shall ask you to give up certain tastes or sacrifice something in your character . . . do some act of charity, of patience, or self-denial . . . or perhaps prove your love by zeal, obedience or abnegation; all such deeds help to fertilize the soil of your soul, which then will be able to produce the flowers and fruit I look for: your self-conquest will obtain light for a sinner . . . your ready patience under provocation will heal the wounds he inflicted on Me, will repair for his offence and expiate his fault . . . a reproof accepted patiently and even with joy will obtain for a sinner blinded by pride the grace to let light penetrate his soul and the courage to beg pardon humbly.

"'All this I will do for you if you will give Me freedom. Then will blossoms grow quickly in your soul, and you will be the consolation of My Heart.

"'Lord, Thou knowest my readiness to let Thee do with me whatsoever Thou wilt. . . . Alas, I have fallen and displeased Thee . . . wilt Thou forgive me once again? I am so wretched and can do no good. . . !

"'Yes, My beloved, even your falls comfort Me. Do not be discouraged, for this act of humility which your fault drew from you has consoled Me more than if you had not fallen. Take courage, go forward steadily, and let Me train you.'

"'All this was present to Me when I instituted the Blessed Sacrament, and My Heart glowed with desire to become the food for just such souls. If I have taken up My abode among men, it is not merely to live among the perfect, but to uphold the weak, and sustain the lowly. I will make them grow and become strong. Their good resolves will be My solace and I will rest in their wretchedness. . . .

"'But are there not some among these chosen souls who will inflict sorrow on Me? . . . For will they all persevere? . . . Such is the cry of grief that breaks from My Heart. . . . I want souls to hear it.

"'Enough for today, Josefa. Farewell. You comfort Me when you entrust yourself entirely to Me. Let Me tell you My secrets for souls, since I cannot speak to them thus every day. Let Me make use of you whilst you are still alive.'"

The very next day, Wednesday, March 7th, Josefa heard the dolorous plaint of His Heart. "Kiss the ground in all humility," He said as was His wont.

She fell down in adoration at His feet, and when she had risen, He spoke: "Write today concerning the pain endured by My Heart, when being constrained by the fire that consumed It, I devised the marvel of love, the Holy Eucharist. And while I looked at those many souls that would feed on this heavenly Bread, I could not but see also the indifference by which so many others . . . consecrated souls . . . priests . . . would wound Me in this Sacrament. There were those who would grow cold . . . gradually yield to routine . . . and worse than routine . . . to weariness and lassitude, and little by little to tepidity. . . . Still, I wait all night and watch in the tabernacle for that soul . . . fervently hoping that she will come and receive Me . . . that she will converse with Me with all the trust of a bride . . . telling Me of her sorrows, her temptations, her sufferings . . . asking My advice and begging for the graces she needs for herself or others. . . . Perhaps she has dependent on her or in her family souls that are in danger and far from Me? . . . 'Come,' I say to her, 'let us discuss everything with perfect freedom. . . . Be concerned about sinners. . . . Offer yourself to make reparation. . . . Promise Me that at least today you will not leave Me alone . . . then see if My Heart is not asking something more of you to comfort It. . . .' This is what I hoped to obtain from that soul and from many another. . . . Yet when she receives Me in Holy Communion, she barely says a word to Me . . . she is distracted, tired or put out . . . her whole mind is absorbed by her occupations . . . her family cares. . . . her acquaintances . . . or maybe anxiety for her health she does not know what to say to Me she is indifferent, bored . . . wishes it were time to go. . . . Is it thus that you receive Me, O soul whom I have chosen and for whom I have watched with all the impatience of love throughout the livelong night?

"'Yes, I yearned for her coming that I might rest in her and share her anxieties. . . . I had prepared fresh graces for her, but she does not want them . . . she has nothing to ask of Me, neither advice nor strength . . . she just complains to herself without so much as addressing Me. . . . It seems then that she has come simply out of routine, to go through a customary formality, or perhaps because no grave sin prevented it. But it is not love nor a true desire for close union with Me that has impelled her coming. Alas, that soul does not possess the delicate love I had hoped to find in her. And priests? Who can express all I expect from each of My priests. . . . They are invested with My own power, that they may forgive sin. . . . I Myself am obedient to their word when they summon Me from Heaven to earth. . . . I am totally surrendered into their hands; they may confine Me to the tabernacle or give Me to the faithful in Holy Communion. . . . They are, so to say, My almoners.

"To each I have entrusted souls that by their preaching, their direction and above all their example, they may guide them in the path of virtue.

"What response do they make? . . . Do they all fulfill Love's mission? . . . Will this My minister at the altar confide the souls of his charges to Me today? Will he make reparation to Me for the offences I receive, the secret of which has been entrusted to him? . . . Will he entreat of Me the strength he needs to carry out in holiness his sacred ministry? . . . zeal to work for the salvation of souls. . . . courage in self-sacrifice, more today than yesterday? Will he give Me all the love I expect . . . and shall I be able to rely entirely on him as on My dear and well-beloved disciple? . . . O what cruel sorrow for My Heart, when I am forced to say: The world wounds Me in My hands and in My feet and it sullies My countenance. . . . My chosen souls and My consecrated religious, My priests, they rend and break My Heart . . . How many priests after giving back grace to many souls are themselves in a state of sin! . . . How many say Mass thus . . . receive Me thus . . . live and die thus!

"Now you know what anguish oppressed Me at the Last Supper when I saw in the midst of the Twelve the first unfaithful apostle . . . and after him so many more who would follow him in the course of the ages.

"The Blessed Sacrament is the invention of Love. It is life and fortitude for souls, a remedy for every fault, and viaticum for the last passage from time to eternity. In it sinners recover life for their souls; tepid souls true warmth; fervent souls, tranquility and the satisfaction of every longing . . . saintly souls, wings to fly towards perfection . . . pure souls sweet honey and rarest sustenance. Consecrated souls find in it a dwelling, their love and their life. In it they will seek and find the perfect exemplar of those sacred and hallowed bonds that unite them inseparably to their heavenly Bridegroom.

"Indeed, O consecrated souls, you will find a perfect symbol of your vow of Poverty in the small, round, light and smooth host; for so must the soul that professes poverty be: no angles, that is to say, no petty natural affections, either for things used nor for her employments, nor for family or country . . . but she must ever be ready to leave, or give up, or change. . . . Her heart must be free, with no attachments whatever. . . .

"This by no means signifies insensibility of heart; no, for the more it loves the more it will preserve the integrity of the vow of Poverty. What is essential for religious souls is first that they should possess nothing without the permission and approbation of Superiors, and secondly, that they should possess and love nothing that they are not ready to give up at the first sign. Later, Josefa, I will tell you the rest."

Several days passed without any mitigation of her suffering state. It seemed to her that several times she had yielded to the violent rebukes of her enemy, and she trembled lest she should have wounded her Master.

"I even lost a Communion," she wrote sorrowfully.

On Laetare Sunday, March 11th, Jesus returned once more, and gave her the full sense of security that she was forgiven.

"Take My Crown and have no fear," He said. "The mercy of God is infinite and never refuses to forgive sinners, and more especially when there is question of a poor little creature like you."

Then alluding to the Communion she had missed:

"O Josefa, if only you had known how I was longing for you to hide Me in your heart!"

She could think of nothing to say to make Him forget that pang.

"You will make amends," He said with the utmost kindness, "by preparing yourself today with very fervent longing for tomorrow's Communion. My Heart is consoled each time you tell Me of this longing . . . and then," He went on, "the spirit of faith and blind obedience always.

"Continue now to write for My souls: Tell them how they will find in the small white Host a perfect symbol of their vow of chastity. For under the species of Bread and Wine the real presence of God lies concealed. Under this veil, I am there, whole and entire, Body, Blood, Soul, and Divinity.

"It is thus that one consecrated to Jesus Christ by the vow of virginity must be hidden under a veil of modesty and simplicity, so that under the appearances of her humanity, a purity like that of the angels may be concealed.

"And understand well, you who form the court of the Immaculate Lamb, that the glory you give Me surpasses incomparably that of the angelic spirits; for they have never experienced the frailties of human nature, and have neither to struggle nor to conquer in order to remain pure.

"You thus acquire a relationship with My Mother, who being a mortal creature was nevertheless of spotless purity . . . subject to all human miseries, yet at every instant of her life absolutely immaculate. She has glorified Me more than all the celestial spirits, and God Himself, drawn by her purity, took flesh of her and dwelt in His creature.

"Further, the soul that is consecrated to Me by the vow of chastity resembles Me, her Creator, as far as it is possible for a human being to do so, for when I clothed Myself in human nature, its miseries not excepted, I lived uncontaminated by the slightest blemish.

"That is how the soul by its vow of chastity becomes a pure white host, which unceasingly renders homage to the Divine Majesty.

"Religious souls, you will find in the Holy Eucharist the model of your vow of obedience.

"For hidden and annihilated there are the greatness and power of God. There, you see Me apparently lifeless, who nevertheless am the life of souls and the support of the world. I can no longer go away or remain, be alone or surrounded: Wisdom, Power, Liberty, all are hidden beneath the Host. . . . The species of bread are the bonds that chain Me and the veil that covers Me.

"In like manner, the vow of obedience is the chain that binds a religious soul, and the veil under which she must disappear, so that she no longer has either will, judgment, choice or liberty, except according to the good pleasure of God as manifested to her by her Superiors."

"Look at My Wounds! Has any one else suffered so much to prove His love?"—Our Lord to Josefa, March 21st, 1923

"It is twenty-two years today," wrote Josefa (Saturday, March 17th, 1923), "since I heard the voice of Jesus for the first time, when I was preparing for my First Communion. I was reminding Him of this during my thanksgiving when suddenly He appeared . . . such loveliness! His garment seemed of gold and His Heart one blaze of fire . . . How can I describe It?"

"'Josefa,' I said to you then, 'I want you to be all Mine.' Today I can say to you: 'You are all Mine.' Then I was preparing to attract you to My Heart . . . today you are imprisoned in It. Come . . . enter and rest therein, since it is your dwelling."

Then He opened His Heart to admit Josefa. . . . "It was like Heaven," she wrote, "and I thought myself no longer on this earth. . . ."

These ineffable moments were of short duration; every time that she enjoyed their strength and peace she knew it to be but a pause between two phases. Such were Heaven's designs.

A few hours later she was at her post of waiting, till it pleased Him to lead her still further into His sorrowful Passion:

"Contemplate Me in the prison where I spent the greater part of the night. The soldiers came and, adding words to injuries, insulted Me, mocked Me, outraged Me, and gave Me blows on My face and on My whole body.

"Tired of their sport, at length they left Me bound and alone in the dark and noisome place, where, seated on a stone, My aching body was cramped with cold.

"Compare the prison with the Tabernacle . . . and especially with the hearts that receive Me.

"In the prison I spent only part of one night but in the Tabernacle, how many days and nights?

"In the prison I was insulted and ill-treated by soldiers who were My enemies. In the Tabernacle most often it is they who call Me their Father who treat Me thus, but how unlike that of children is the treatment! . . .

"In the prison I endured cold, sleeplessness, hunger and thirst, pain, shame, solitude, and desertion. And there passed before My mind's eye all the tabernacles where in the course of ages I should lack the shelter of love . . . the icy-cold hearts that would be as hard and unfeeling as the stones of the prison floor were to My numbed and wounded body.

"And how often should I wait for this or that other soul to visit Me in the Blessed Sacrament and receive Me into his heart . . . how many nights should I spend longing for his coming . . . but he would let business or carelessness or anxiety for his health get the better of him . . . and he would not come!

"How often should I hunger for souls . . . for their fidelity . . . for their generosity . . . would they satisfy that eager hunger by a little victory over self or by a slight mortification? . . . Would they comfort Me in My sorrow by their tenderness and compassion? . . . In some hard moment would they endure the pain . . . neglect . . . scorn . . . opposition . . . grief of soul or family . . . would they come to Me and say: 'This I offer Thee to console Thy sadness, to keep Thee company in Thy solitude.' O! if they would thus unite themselves to Me, with what peace would they face difficulties . . . how much fortitude they would win and how they would gladden My Heart!

"In the prison what shame I felt at the obscene words of those around Me . . . and My distress was increased by the thought that like words would one day fall from lips I love.

"When blows and buffets were rained upon Me by the filthy hands of the soldiery, it recalled to My mind how often those who would receive Me into hearts fouled by unrepented sin would shower reiterated blows on Me by habitual and willed sin.

"And in the prison when they pushed Me and let Me fall to the ground bound and helpless, so many were present to My mind who would prefer a moment's satisfaction to Me, would load Me with chains by their ingratitude, would push Me back and again cause Me to fall, by leaving Me alone.

"O you who are consecrated to Me, draw near to the Bridegroom of your souls in His prison. Gaze steadfastly upon Him during that night of pain and see that sorrow continued in the loneliness of countless tabernacles and the coldness of many hearts.

"If you are desirous of proving your sympathy, open your hearts and let Me find a prison therein. . . .

"There bind Me with chains of love . . . there clothe Me with loving attentions. . . . Appease My hunger by your generosity. . . . Assuage My thirst by your zeal. . . . Comfort Me in My sorrow by keeping Me faithful company and wiping away My shame by your purity and uprightness of intention.

"If you wish Me to take My rest in you, prepare for My coming by acts of self-denial . . . master your imagination and calm the tumult of your passions . . . then in the stillness of your soul you will hear My voice speaking gently within you: Today you are My repose, but for all eternity I shall be your rest. . . . Tenderly and with love you have harbored Me in the prison of your heart. I shall be your reward exceeding great and you will never regret any sacrifice you have made for Me during your life!"

"Love humbles Itself. . . . Love surrenders Itself" —Our Lord to Josefa, March 29th, 1923

"Josefa, today is My great day, the day of

Love. . . . Its feastday," said Our Lord on the morning of Holy Thursday.

She was at prayer in her cell and suddenly He came as on the preceding day, with a Heart surrounded with flames. She renewed her vows and fell on her face in adoration before Him. He spoke:

"Today is the day on which I give Myself to souls, that I may be for them just what they wish: If they will look on Me as their Father, I shall be a Father to them. . . . If they desire Me as their Beloved, I shall be their Beloved. . . . If they need strength, I will be their Strength, and if they long to console Me, I will let them console Me. . . . All I want is to give Myself to them . . . and to fill them with graces prepared for them. . . . I cannot withhold them any longer. What, Josefa, shall I be to you?"

"My All, Lord, for I am nothing!"

Tranquil peace and gratitude filled Josefa's heart, and so she went to Mass, then to Holy Communion. On returning to her place, she at once renewed the complete offering of her whole person to her good and beloved Master, definitely abandoning herself into His hands for ever. Jesus ratified the offering:

"It is on account of your nothingness and utter misery that you must let Me kindle your heart's fire, consume and destroy it. You surely know that 'nothing' and 'misery' cannot resist . . ."

Josefa spent the whole day under the power of "Love that gives" . . . "and Love that humbles Itself before Its own" . . . She would hear these words from Our Lord's lips while in the silence and recollection of that day she lived through the ceremonies of religious life, the last actions, the last outpourings of the love of our Savior among His own.

At about four in the afternoon, Josefa was at prayer in her cell near a statue of Our Blessed Lady and was thinking over the mysterious words of Jesus, when He Himself appeared.

"Yes, Josefa, I did indeed say that Love gives Itself to Its own and it is true. . . . Come, draw near My Heart and enter in, and taste and see what its overwhelming emotions are."

"'Love gives Itself as food to Its own and this food is the substance which gives them their life and sustains them.

"'Love humbles Itself before Its own . . . and in so doing raises them to the highest dignity.

"'Love surrenders Itself in totality, It gives in profusion and without reserve. With enthusiasm, with vehemence It is sacrificed, It is immolated, It is given for those It loves. . . . The Holy Eucharist is love to the extreme of folly.'"

It looked as if Our Lord at that moment was unable to restrain the burning effusions of His

Heart; then His voice changed and He spoke with gravity, saying: "This love will lead Me to My death! . . . "

Then, turning to Josefa, He addressed her directly: "Today you are sustained, consoled, and strengthened by love; tomorrow, Josefa, you will accompany Me to Calvary and suffer with Me."

"Then I saw no one but Jesus alone, extending His hand, He said, with eyes raised to Heaven: 'May men adore the Father. May they love the Son. May they let themselves be possessed by the Holy Spirit, and may the Blessed Trinity abide in them.'"

Then, He fixed His eyes on Josefa: "O! if you could but see the beauty of a soul in grace. But such beauty is invisible to mortal eyes, Josefa. Look rather with eyes of faith, and realizing the value of souls, consecrate yourself to giving this glory to the Blessed Trinity, by gaining many souls in which the Triune God may find a dwelling."

Jesus continued instructing her in very simple language: "Every soul can be instrumental in this sublime work. . . . Nothing great is required, the smallest acts suffice: a step taken, a straw picked up, a glance restrained, a service rendered, a cordial smile . . . all these offered to Love are in reality of great profit to souls and draw down floods of grace on them. No need to remind you of the fruits of prayer, of sacrifice, of any act offered to expiate the sins of mankind . . . to obtain for them the grace of purification, that they too may become fitting sanctuaries for the indwelling of the Blessed Trinity."

"All My longing is to set hearts on fire . . . to set the whole world on fire"—Our Lord to Josefa, June 12th, 1923

The time had now come, when according to the divine will, Josefa was to transmit the desires of the Sacred Heart to the Bishop of Poitiers. Very gravely Our Lord prepared her for the continuation of His Message on Sunday, June 10th. It looked as if He wanted all possible security for His words, while at the same time He reassured and strengthened His frail intermediary, Josefa.

"While I was writing in my cell this morning, Jesus came," noted Josefa. "His wonderful beauty was enhanced by the majesty and sovereign power that the tone of His voice expressed. 'Josefa,' He said, 'humble yourself, and make an act of entire submission to God's holy will.'

"I prostrated myself in adoration before Him and He continued: 'Offer My Heart the profound, tender, and generous love of yours.'

"This I did from the very depths of my being. Then He was silent, as if waiting for something further. . . .

"I renewed my vows. I told Him that I belong to Him and that I am ready to do whatever He wills. I think that was what He was waiting for, for then He said: 'As I have triumphed over your heart and your love, you will not refuse Me anything, will you?'

"No, dear Lord, I am Thine for evermore.'

"'Then tomorrow I will come and tell you what in the first place you are to communicate to the Bishop.'"

Josefa was filled with fear. "I was unable to hide it," she wrote, "and I told Him how frightened I feel at the mere thought of it."

"'You need have no fear,'" He replied. "My Heart is watching over you, and besides, it is for souls."

This assurance somewhat allayed her anxiety.

"When I think of having to speak of all those things to His Lordship the Bishop, I am very frightened," she noted, "but I am certain that Jesus will give me the courage I need.

"That evening, when Jesus came to forgive my sins, I again told Him of my fear.

"'You will have to suffer, Josefa, but it is for souls, and did I not suffer Myself to redeem and save them?'"

Our Blessed Lord stimulated her generosity by laying such motives before her, and her close union with His Sacred Heart also helped her to accept all that was to be demanded of her.

On Monday, June 11th, in the quiet of her thanksgiving after Communion, something of the vastness of His plans was revealed to Josefa.

"Why are you afraid?" He said. "Do you not know that I love you and am watching over you? It is all for souls. . . . They must know Me . . . they must love Me more. . . . Children ought to make their father known. You are My well-loved daughters, specially chosen, that through you I may be revealed and that My Heart may be glorified. You need not fear, for I am strong and will make you strong; I am Love and will sustain you. . . . I will not abandon you."

A few minutes later Our Lord rejoined her in her cell. "I am now about to tell you, Josefa, the first thing that you are to tell the Bishop. Kiss the ground!"

She renewed her vows and prostrated herself at His feet. Then Jesus began to speak and Josefa wrote:

"I am *Love!* My Heart can no longer contain its devouring flames. I love souls so dearly that I have sacrificed My life for them.

"It is this love that keeps Me a prisoner in the

tabernacle. For nearly twenty centuries I have dwelt there, night and day, veiled under the species of Bread and concealed in the small white Host, bearing through love, neglect, solitude, contempt, blasphemies, outrages, sacrileges. . . .

"For love of souls, I instituted the Sacrament of Penance, that I might forgive them, not once or twice, but as often as they need to recover grace. There I wait for them, longing to wash away their sins, not in water, but in My Blood.

"How often in the course of the ages have I, in one way or another, made known My love for men: I have shown them how ardently I desire their salvation. I have revealed My Heart to them. This devotion has been as light cast over the whole earth, and today is a powerful means of gaining souls, and so of extending My kingdom.

"Now, I want something more, for if I long for love in response to My own, this is not the only return I desire from souls: I want them all to have confidence in My mercy, to expect all from My clemency, and never to doubt My readiness to forgive.

"I am God, but a God of love! I am a Father, but a Father full of compassion and never harsh. My Heart is infinitely holy but also infinitely wise, and, knowing human frailty and infirmity, stoops to poor sinners with infinite mercy.

"I love those who after a first fall come to Me

for pardon. . . . I love them still more when they beg pardon for their second sin, and should this happen again, I do not say a million times but a million million times, I still love them and pardon them, and I will wash in My Blood their last as fully as their first sin.

"Never shall I weary of repentant sinners, nor cease from hoping for their return, and the greater their distress, the greater My welcome. Does not a father love a sick child with special affection? Are not his care and solicitude greater? So is the tenderness and compassion of My Heart more abundant for sinners than for the just.

"This is what I wish all to know. I will teach sinners that the mercy of My Heart is inexhaustible. Let the callous and indifferent know that My Heart is a fire which will enkindle them, because I love them. To devout and saintly souls I would be the Way, that making great strides in perfection, they may safely reach the harbour of eternal beatitude. Lastly, of consecrated souls, priests and religious, My elect and chosen ones, I ask, once more, all their love and that they should not doubt Mine, but above all that they should trust Me and never doubt My mercy, It is so easy to trust completely in My Heart!"

Here Jesus ended His appeal. He gave Josefa a few indications to be transmitted to her director, who was to lay the whole matter before the Bishop, and reading in Josefa's soul all the anxiety she felt: "Why, why do you fear?" and tenderly He soothed her. "You know that I love you.... You know, too, that it is for souls and for My glory. Do not be troubled.... Just carry out My directions and give Me all the time that I want."

"Soon the never-ending day will dawn." —Our Lord to Josefa, December 12th, 1923

"That will be our work in Heaven, Josefa; to teach souls how to live united to Me, not as if I were far away, but in them, because by grace I dwell in them, and in Holy Communion, My Sacred Humanity becomes, so to speak, incarnate in them.

"If My chosen ones lived thus united to Me and really knew Me, how much good they would be able to do to many poor souls who are far from Me and do not know Me.

"When My chosen ones are closely united to My Heart, they will realize how often I am offended . . . they will understand My feelings. . . . Then they will comfort Me and repair for sinners, and full of trust in Me, they will ask pardon and obtain grace for the world."

A PRACTICAL SUGGESTION

The closing of churches during the day is quite common today and the reason for it is a valid one: the danger of theft or vandalism.

A solution for keeping them open that has been tried and found to work is the formation of a volunteer group of parishioners who promise to make a visit for at least a half-hour once a week, on the same day and at the same time each week. By grouping the half-hour periods and stringing them out successively, provision is made for one of the "relay team" to be in church all the time it is open. It would take only four volunteers to keep a church open two hours on a particular day. Twenty volunteers could provide adorers two hours a day for five days. This project, obviously, is also recommended for parishes where churches are open during the day.

If the time when the volunteer adorers are to be in church were publicized in the parish bulletin, parishioners unable to commit themselves to a definite time, would be able to make a visit at their own convenience.

This system leads to several other possibilities:

some might volunteer to be responsible for an hour instead of a half-hour; some might volunteer to come on more than one day; some might be willing to serve on a stand-by basis, i.e., be willing to replace an adorer unable to keep his or her appointment. In most cases, it would take just one apostolic person on the phone to get together a group that would keep Our Lord company for at least a few hours a day, as representatives of the whole parish, that is, for those who cannot be there and/or who do not want to be there.

Jesus has made Himself a Prisoner in the tabernacle. But, by keeping our churches locked during the day, we have in effect placed Him in solitary confinement! Let us no longer offer Him indifference, but love and reparation-and surely He will not be outdone in generosity.

THE WAY OF DIVINE LOVE. Sr. Josefa Menéndez. 570 pp. Paperbound. Imprimatur. One of the greatest spiritual classics of all time. A large part of this book comes from Our Lord Himself, as He reveals the secrets of His love for man to this humble 20th-century nun. This book makes lasting devotees of its readers, for Our Lord Himself promised in this book, "I tell you once more that grace will accompany My words and those who make them known. Truth will triumph and peace will reign over souls and the world." Her description of Hell, written under obedience, is alone worth the price of the book.

TAN · BOOKS

TAN Books was founded in 1967 to preserve the spiritual, intellectual and liturgical traditions of the Catholic Church. At a critical moment in history TAN kept alive the great classics of the Faith and drew many to the Church. In 2008 TAN was acquired by Saint Benedict Press. Today TAN continues its mission to a new generation of readers.

From its earliest days TAN has published a range of booklets that teach and defend the Faith. Through partnerships with organizations, apostolates, and mission-minded individuals, well over 10 million TAN booklets have been distributed.

More recently, TAN has expanded its publishing with the launch of Catholic calendars and daily planners—as well as Bibles, fiction, and multimedia products through its sister imprints Catholic Courses (catholiccourses.com) and Saint Benedict Press (saintbenedictpress.com).

Today TAN publishes over 500 titles in the areas of theology, prayer, devotions, doctrine, Church history, and the lives of the saints. TAN books are published in multiple languages and found throughout the world in schools, parishes, bookstores and homes.

For a free catalog, visit us online at
TANBooks.com

Or call us toll-free at
(800) 437-5876